Inspirational Time with Ashley Blanshaw

A little Devotional Book inspired from my series and my podcast

Season 1

By Ashley Katisha Blanshaw

Introduction

Inspirational Time with Ashley Blanshaw was created and inspired by my podcast series, *Ashley's Inspirations* on Facebook Live. I began this podcast because I want to encourage and minister to you. No matter what you are going through, God is fighting for and working it out for you.

During these times, we are living in a pandemic called Covid-19. As a result, a lot has changed. So many obstacles and struggles have arisen. There are times you must wonder why so many things are happening. In my series, *Inspirational Time*, I always mention that 2nd Timothy 1:7 reads, *"God didn't give us the spirit of fear but of love and power and a sound mind."* I want to remind you in this little devotional book of what the Bible declares in 2nd Chronicles 20:15, *"…for the battle is not your, but God's."*

Always encourage yourself that in spite of what you are going through, you are an overcomer. You will get through this because God will take care of you. Sometimes it is going to be hard and the road is going to get tough, but King David wrote these words in Psalm 27:14, *"Wait on the Lord, be of good courage, and he shall strengthen your heart."* Hold onto your faith and keep praying; *God has everything under control.*

I also want this little devotional book to encourage and remind you that we serve a God Who supplies all of our needs (Philippians 4:19). God has you in the palm of His hands; just trust and believe in Him. In His time, God will fix every situation and work out every problem you are facing.

Chapter 1

God is supplying and will restore you seven times greater for your losses!

Scriptures: Philippians 4: 19 and Psalms 23

God is going to restore every blessing, miracle, overflow, healing, and deliverance greater than what the devil stole from you. God is going to give it back to you greater and better than ever. God is going to give it back to you double and triple-fold. Every dream, goal, vision, and plan you had that had been lost—plans you thought had failed, and that the devil, bullies, and naysayers said would never come to pass—God will return them to you greater and better than ever before. Believe it in your heart; receive it in your heart. Believe that God will do it for you, your family, your children, your friends, your church family, and your pastor.

There will be times when you feel like giving up, but always encourage yourself. Tell yourself, *"I refuse to give up and I refuse to quit because God has a purpose, a plan, and a vision for me to carry forth. I will not stay stuck in this problem I am currently going through. I refuse to let this situation get the best of me. This obstacle will not hold me and pull me down anymore. I will overcome this! Regardless of the trials I am facing right now, I am going to be restored, delivered, and healed because I serve a God Who is a Provider, a Healer, a Deliverer, a Strong Tower, a Miracle Worker, and a Way-Maker."*

Receive it right now! God is going to make a way for you and He is working everything out for you. Believe that God is fixing every situation, obstacle, struggle, trouble, and problem that you are in right now. Declare and decree this over your life right now: *"After this pandemic we will have complete victory! I'm getting ready for my miracle and blessing overflow. I'm getting ready for greater comebacks in my life. I'm getting ready for something amazing, marvelous, wonderful, and great to happen in my life. I'm coming out of this, better and stronger than ever. Giant and greater leaps towards my destiny, my dreams, and my goals are happening in my life."*

God is doing something greater in your life. God is doing something special in your life. Receive it right now. Claim your miracle now. Claim your blessing now. Claim your victory now. Claim your breakthrough now. Claim your healing now. Claim your deliverance now. Restoration is coming. Acceleration is coming. Miracles, Signs, and wonders are on the way. Believe and receive it right now. God is supplying and restoring you SEVEN TIMES GREATER for your losses.

Chapter 2

I Won't Let the Devil Win Because God Is Fighting for Me

James 4:7, Psalms 120: 1&2 and Isaiah 54:17

I want to encourage you that God is fighting for you. Always know that this battle is not yours, it is The Lord's. I want you to know you are going to make it through the trials and tribulations you are facing right now. Know that all the negative comments and negative words the devil, the bullies, and the naysayers have told you is nothing but a lie. Encourage yourself by believing you will receive everything that God says about you. Tell yourself that you are not worrying about anything the enemy told you. Encourage yourself by declaring that you are more than a conqueror; you are a champion, a winner, victorious, an overcomer and a survivor. Also, declare to yourself that you are healed, restored, and delivered.

You've been crying long enough; you have given up too much. You've felt like *"throwing in the towel."* The devil has been messing with your mind. The devil also has been messing with you at night, interrupting your sleep. The devil has been attacking your mind, body, love ones, your marriages/relationships, your finances and your job.

I mention this in every episode of *Ashley's Inspirations*: Sometimes situations and problems you are going through make you want to question if you are the only one the devil is attacking. However, I remind my listeners that the reason why is that God is doing something greater, bigger, and better in your life. For that reason, I want to encourage you that this is your season of winning, greatness, happiness, miracles, signs, and wonders. This is also your season of miracle blessing overflows. This is your season of greater, bigger, and better things; your season of greater comebacks with upgrades and increases. This is also your season of greater financial blessings, open doors, open opportunities, and increase in ministries and businesses. Tell yourself that I am coming out of this stronger and better than before. Declare to yourself, *"I refuse to back down and back out. I won't let these trials and tribulations or these problems and obstacles get the best of me. God sees the best in me, so I won't let these negative comments or words get me down."*

The Bible declares that the enemy that you have seen, you will see no more because when the devil comes to plan your failure and your downfall, God will *"flip the script,"* cancel the plans of the enemy, and turn it into a success and a blessing. Every negative distraction, roadblock, and evil plan the devil has put in your path, God is going to stop it. God will also destroy every yoke the devil is trying to attach to you. For every dream and goal the devil said would never reach successful completion, I want to encourage you that with the help of the Lord, your dreams and goals WILL REACH SUCCESSFUL COMPLETION!

God has called and chosen you to fulfill the purpose and plan He has for you. In Episode 12 of *Ashley's Inspirations* and Chapter 1 of this inspirational book, I stated that God is supplying and restoring what you lost, and it is going to be seven times greater and better than ever. So, encourage yourself! Announce to yourself, *"I won't let the devil win because God is fighting for me!"*

Chapter 3

Keep Fulfilling Your Purpose

Psalms 20:4, Romans 8:28, Philippians 4:19 and Ephesians 6:13

God is doing amazing and wonderful things in your life. Keep fulfilling your destiny, your purpose, and the plan that God has for you. Keep focusing and seeking to do the Will of God. Keep fulfilling your destiny and reaching toward your dreams and goals. Don't let any obstacles, struggles, roadblocks, situations, or troubles stop you from fulfilling your purpose.

Psalms 20:4 reads, "*May He grant you according to your heart's desire, And fulfill all your purpose.*" It means whatever you need, God has you covered. God is going to supply everything you need. At times it is going to be hard for you to fulfill your destiny and purpose because of the tribulations that you are going through. Other times, the enemy is going to attempt to sow negative thoughts into your mind, which may cause you to lose sight of God. The enemy is also going to try to make you lose focus of your destiny, your dreams, your goals, and your purpose. All of these distractions may cause you to think about giving up.

However, I want you to encourage yourself and declare and decree these words over your life, "*No matter what I am going through right now, I am going to continue to keep fulfilling my purpose and my destiny*".

Here is a life application: In 2009 one of my spiritual fathers from my home church encouraged me to become a Christian, join the church, and begin my spiritual journey. I kept questioning why I should, considering all of the struggles, obstacles, and negative events I was going through at the time. Looking back, I now realize that God was calling and choosing me to fulfill His purpose and plan.

In my Facebook Live series, *Ashley's Inspirations*, I talked about the life of King David. Although he was verbally discouraged by his own family, King David fulfilled the purpose God had for him to defeat the giant Goliath (1st Samuel 17).

Encourage yourself by declaring, *"I don't care what the devil said because whatever he says is NOTHING BUT A LIE. I believe and receive everything that God says about me. I am more than a conqueror. I am the head and NOT the tail. I am above and NOT beneath. I am victorious. I am a winner and a champion!"*

Encourage yourself. You have a purpose and a destiny that God has given you. God has chosen you to fulfill that purpose and no demon, devil, bully, doubter, roadblock, negative word/comment, distraction, obstacle, or struggle is going to stop you. Always know and remember that God has you covered. In God's time, things are going to happen for you.

Chapter 4

Don't Get Discouraged; God Is Working It Out For You!

Ephesians 6:13; Job 29: 4; Psalms 46: 1 and 10; and John 14:1

Sometimes as a follower of God and as a Christian on this journey, life will get difficult because of the obstacles and troubles that are coming your way. You have been fasting and praying, but at times you will question if God is really on your side. You have been searching for answers, but you are feeling as if you are getting nowhere. You are trying to find a way out of your dilemma. When situations and obstacles become overbearing, it often makes you question why you seem to be the only one the devil is attacking.

During my Facebook Live series, *Ashley's Inspirations,* I shared that the reason you are going through is because God is doing something special and amazing in your life that the devil doesn't want you to have. Nevertheless, I want to encourage you that what the devil meant for evil, God will turn it around for your good (Genesis 50:20).

In the Gospel of John, Chapter 14, verse 1, Jesus said, *"Don't let your heart be troubled, Believe in God, believe also in me."* This means that you shouldn't get discouraged; just trust in God. Believe in Him, have faith in Him, and pray to Him. Don't allow your problems and troubles to keep you from praying, because God is your refuge and your strength (Psalm 46:1). When you are at a place where you are feeling weak — when you feel like giving up and when the devil is trying to you knock you down — all you have to do is call on the name of the Lord, and He will answer your prayer. God will heal and strengthen you. Storms may rise, troubles may increase, and situations may become overbearing. Nevertheless, always turn to God in prayer.

In Episode One from my series, *Ashley's Inspirations* (on Facebook Live) I discussed the 20th chapter of 2nd Kings. Verse 1 records that King Hezekiah was sick and near death. The Prophet Isaiah went to him with bad news; he declared, *"Thus says the Lord; Set your house in order, for you shall die; you shall not recover."* However, that news did not stop King Hezekiah from turning to God in prayer. Verse 2 reads, *"Then Hezekiah turned his face to the wall and prayed to the Lord."* King Hezekiah prayed because he believed God was going to work it out for him.

In another episode from my series, *Ashley's Inspirations*, I shared a passage of scripture from 1st Samuel Chapter 1. In this passage of scripture, we find the two wives of Elkanah: Hannah and Peninnah. Peninnah had given birth to children, but Hannah could not bear children because God had closed her womb. Although bearing a child seemed impossible, it did not stop Hannah from having faith and praying. Hannah believed that God was going to hear her prayer, perform a miracle, and open her womb. Hannah kept the faith, prayed to the Lord, and the miracle arrived. She was blessed with a son, whom she named Samuel and dedicated to the Lord.

In another episode from my series, I talked about the relationship between Ruth and Naomi. Ruth—who was a young woman—didn't have to stay with her mother-in-law after Ruth's husband died. Yet when Naomi tried to send Ruth away, Ruth said, *"Where you go, I will go, your people shall be my people and your God shall be my God"* (Ruth 1:16). Ruth had faith that God would bless her and Naomi as well, which He did. Ruth later married Boaz, a man of great wealth. Ruth conceived and gave birth to son named

Obed, who was the grandfather of King David. Ruth became the great-grandmother of

King David!

So, I want to encourage you that what you are facing may be discouraging, hard,

impossible, scary, troubling, and difficult, but like King Hezekiah, *"turn your face to the*

wall" and pray. Things are going to work out for the good, because God has everything

under control! God is going to do it for you.

Chapter 5

Keep Praying, keep having Faith!
God is answering your prayers and joy is coming!

Nehemiah 8:10, Job 22: 27, Psalms 139: 14, Psalms 94: 19, Romans 12:12

Life may sometimes be difficult and discouraging, but I encourage you to keep praying. It might be a struggle, but keep praying. You might want to ask the question, *"When am I going to make it through this?"* You want to know if God hears you or is willing to answer your prayers. There are going to be times when you are going to be saying to yourself, *"I have been praying and fasting but I am still not seeing any results."*

I want to remind you that God is an on-time God. The songwriter declared, *"He may not come when you want him, but He'll be there right on time."* In Psalms 27, verse 14, King David wrote, *"Wait on The Lord, be of good courage, and he shall strengthen thy heart."*

Expect the devil to come and attempt to discourage you and try to make you worried; but, I want to remind you that God is listening to your prayers. God hears your prayers. Just keep praying and don't worry. Everything is going to be alright. Everything is working for your good. Situations that arise may be horrible at first, but always know that God is on your side because it says in Philippians 4: 19, "*I can do all things through Christ who strengthens me.*"

Look the devil in his face and say, "*Devil, I don't know what you are trying to do but your evil plans will not work. I made a decision that no matter what struggle, obstacle, situation, problem, and trouble I am going through, I am going to keep rejoicing and praising the Lord. I serve a God Who is a Healer, a Waymaker, a Deliverer, and a Miracle Worker, and my God is going work everything out and make a way for me!*"

GET READY, because your miracle is on the way, your blessing is on the way, your breakthrough is on the way. Your healing is on the way and your deliverance is the way. Believe that today.

Receive right now that God is doing a new thing in your life. Receive right now that God is doing greater and bigger things in your life. Just keep praying and never give up, because God is with you.

GOD IS WORKING EVERYTHING OUT FOR YOU!

Chapter 6

Get Ready: Your Miracle And Blessing Overflow Is On The Way!

Exodus 15:13 and Isaiah 40:29

Always know that God is working a miracle and blessing overflow in your life. God is going do it seven times greater, and better than ever. No devil, bully, naysayer, or negative comments and words can stop you from receiving your miracle and blessing overflow that God has for you. I suggest that you get ready because God is doing a new thing in your life. I know it might be hard, but get ready because God is doing a miracle in your life. A blessing is coming and it is going to happen for you. Don't get discouraged; don't quit. Don't you back down because God is working out every situation, every problem, fixing every obstacle, every struggle, and healing every sickness that you are going through right now.

Stay focused and on track. Don't let any negative distractions cause you to lose focus and sight of God. God has everything under control and will turn your situation in to a miracle and your obstacle into a blessing. Receive it right now; claim it right now.

Go back and re-read Chapter 4 and the miracle of a baby boy born to a barren woman named Hannah. I want to encourage you that the situation you are going through right now may challenging or painful, but keep praying and having faith, because God is working a miracle in your life.

I know it's hard, but don't stop praying. I know it's tough, but don't stop believing. Everything is going to work out for your good. Trust in the Lord and never doubt because God will take care of you. Encourage yourself by declaring, *"I refuse and won't let the devil win because God is fighting for me. I might be going through right now but I am going to keep on holding on and being strong because I will overcome this. I will be healed from this."* Decree and Declare it right now! Declare and Decree over the lives of your children, your family, your church family, your pastors, your love ones, and yourself that miracles and blessing overflows are on the way. What we are about to receive will be seven times greater and better than ever, because from Episode 12 from my series *Ashlie's Inspirations,* God is supplying and restoring what all of us have lost. Every miracle, blessing, joy, love, peace, happiness and deliverance that the devil stole, God is going to give back to us double and triple fold. The Apostle Paul wrote these words in Philippians 4:19, *"And my God shall supply all your need according to His riches in glory by Christ Jesus."*

I love the song by the amazing Tasha Cobbs Leonard entitled, *"I'm Getting Ready;"* I am declaring and decreeing this over my life, too, that my miracle and blessing overflow is on its way and it's going to be seven times greater and better than ever!

Something amazing, marvelous, wonderful is going to happen in your life. God is doing something special, great, and amazing in your life. Hold on and be strong. Keep having faith and keep praying. God is working a miracle and blessing overflow for you and in your life.

Chapter 7

Don't get Discouraged because Your Help is on The Way!

Psalms 91, Psalms 121, Psalms 37:40, John 14:1, Joshua 1:6, 2 Timothy 1:7

Life's obstacles and struggles can make you feel discouraged, make you worry, and make you question everything. At times they make you want to quit and walk away from everything. However, I mention in every episode of *Ashley's Inspirations* the importance of not allowing negative distractions to stop you from receiving the great things that God has for you and what He is doing in your life.

There are going to be times when the devil will try to put negative distractions in your way; to make you lose focus of your goals and lose sight of God. I want to encourage you that with God, everything is going to be alright. Don't worry because your help is on the way. Don't quit or give up because your help is on the way. Don't you back down because your help is on the way, your healing is on the way, and your breakthrough is on the way. Your miracle and blessing overflow are on the way; signs, wonders and your deliverance are on the way. Receive and claim it right now that your help is on the way. Declare to yourself that you are refusing to be stuck in the situation that you are in. Declare to yourself that God is going to bring me out of that situation that I am in.

In every episode of *Ashley's Inspirations*, I declared, *"The battle is NOT YOURS, it is THE LORD'S."* There are going to be times you may find yourself in trouble, but always remember the words of the song written by the late Reverend Timothy Wright, *"I'm So Glad Trouble Don't Last Always."*

There is also an old song that declares, *"He may not come when you want him but He'll be there right on time."* King David wrote these words, recorded in Psalms 27: 14, *"Wait on the Lord, be strong and take heart and wait for the Lord"* (NIV).

So, I want to encourage you that in the midst of your sickness, broken relationship, problems on your job, financial difficulties, obstacles and struggles, God is with you. God is going to bring you out of whatever that you are going through. Your situation might be difficult, but encourage yourself that trouble don't last always and that you are getting ready to receive your breakthrough. Encourage yourself that you are going to make it through this challenging season and enter into your season of winning and success. There are going to be times when the devil will try to put distractions and roadblocks in front of you that will cause you to want to give up, but I encourage you to focus on God. Everything He said will come to pass. Everything is going to be alright because your help is on the way. Just trust in God, believe, and continue to have faith.

Chapter 8

You will Overcome This,

You Will Be Healed From This,

And You Will Be Delivered From This

Isaiah 53:5, Psalms 18:17,19, 48, Psalms 24:4, 54:7 and Proverbs 14: 26, 18:10

I want to encourage you that no matter what you are going through right now, you will overcome this, you will be healed from this, and you will be delivered from this. No matter what battle, addiction, sickness, obstacle, trouble, struggle, trial, and tribulation that you are going through right now, you will be delivered from this.

Always know that you are going to come out this, whether it is a battle or addiction, sickness or problem. Always know and encourage yourself that you are coming out of this stronger and better.

Also, encourage yourself that you are coming out completely healed and delivered. Just hold on and be strong because God is making a way for you. Don't get discouraged. Sometimes it might be tough, sometimes it might be hard, and sometimes you want to quit on everything but I want to encourage you NOT to give up. Make the decision that you will NOT lose sight of God; you will NOT lose faith; and you will NOT stop praying, because God is working everything out for you.

Sometimes what you are going through right now—perhaps a bad breakup, a financial problem or a situation at your job—can make you want to question everything. You may find yourself saying, *"When am I going to get out of this?"* or asking God, *"When is my miracle, my blessing and my healing going to come?"* You may have been going through problem after problem, bad breakup after bad breakup, discouragement after discouragement, lie after lie, struggle after struggle, obstacle after obstacle, battle after battle, addiction after addiction, and situation after situation, and you are always wondering and saying, *"When will this be over? When will I find joy, peace, and happiness?"* Let me encourage you right now: God is fixing it right now and God is fighting for you.

It is sometimes hard to stay in the faith and keep praying when you have been dealing with bullies who harass you, and naysayers who constantly criticize you, and so-called friends who cheat on you and accuse you of being someone who you are not.

Some of you have also been dealing with people who have labeled you with negative words and comments. Others have blamed you, hurt you, and said that you would never amount to anything, and that your dreams and goals will never come to pass because of your past experiences. I want somebody to look the devil in his face and say to him right now, *"Devil, everything that you said to me is NOTHING BUT A LIE BECAUSE I SERVE A GOD THAT SEES THE BEST IN ME, I SERVE A GOD THAT WILL HELP ME OVERCOME THIS, AND THAT WILL DELIVER ME AND WILL HEAL ME FROM THIS."* Tell the devil right now that in spite of this pandemic, in spite of Covid-19, in spite of the battle, addiction, struggle, obstacle, trouble, and problem, I am going to make it through this.

Declare and decree this over your life: I am getting ready to have total and complete victory after this. I am still getting ready for my miracle and blessing overflow, breakthrough, healing, and deliverance. Always know that you serve a God Who is our Healer, Deliverer, Savior, Provider, Strong Tower, and Helper!

Keep staying in the faith! Don't stop praying because you will be healed and delivered!

Chapter 9

God is Fighting for you and He will deliver you

Psalms 18: 17 &19, Psalms 91, Jeremiah 1:8 and Jeremiah 20:13

During the course of life, you will get in to place where you will to question everything and begin to wonder when am you are going to get out of the situation that you am in. You ask yourself, *"When am I going to be delivered from this obstacle, sickness, and struggle that I am in?"*

In every episode of *Ashley's Inspirations*, I mention the question many of you are asking yourself, *"Why is the devil attacking me so much?"* Sometimes the situation takes its toll and it becomes too much for you to bear. However, I always remind everyone that all this is happening because something greater, bigger and better is taking place in your life.

God Is doing something special in your life, so the enemy is going to be really busy. I want to encourage you that greater and bigger things are happening for you. God has a greater and bigger and better comeback for you, with upgrades in miracles, signs and wonders. Upgrades in overflows, blessings, open doors and opportunities. Just hold on and be strong. Stay in the faith and keep praying because God is fighting for you. He will deliver you.

Episode 12 from *Ashley's Inspirations* has been the theme for this year; you need to believe and receive that after this pandemic, you are going to have total victory. How many of you also believe and receive that God is supplying and restoring what you lost? As I declared in Chapter 1, can you believe that God is going restore you seven times greater for your losses? Can you believe that God is going to restore every miracle, blessing, joy, happiness, overflow that the devil stole from you? Just trust and know that God is on your side.

There are times you are going to have moments of wanting to give up, but I want to encourage you that God is your Keeper, Provider, and Protector. He will protect you from all danger and from all harm. He is a Waymaker, Healer, and a Deliverer. At this very moment, God is working out every problem and situation you are facing. God is going to bring you out of that problem you are in.

Here is another life application: Life was hard for me, and there were times I felt like giving up. I thought about quitting, but I now realize that I was repeatedly being attacked by the devil because God was doing something greater, bigger, and better in my life. God is supplying what I lost, and God is restoring me seven times greater, bigger, and better! God has a greater and better comeback for me with upgrades in miracles, signs, wonders, overflows, blessings, open doors and opportunities.

I also learned that a road or a journey to recovery and to success will not be easy, but if I keep praying, having faith in God, and keep seeking God, He will help me make it through whatever situation I am facing. So, I want to let you know that a journey to recovery is not going to be easy; it is going to be tough sometime, but if you keep staying focused and keep moving forward and never look back, you will be successful. God has chosen you to fulfill the purpose, the plan, the vision, and the destiny that He has for you. Believe and receive it right now. Declare to yourself that you will be healed from your illness and be restored from this. Say to yourself, "*In spite of what I am going through right now, I am going to keep on praying and worshipping God because God is going to bring me out of this. I will get through this. I will going to have total complete victory after this. God is doing great things for me and I am ready to receive it".*

Get ready for a manifestation that is about to take place in your life. Are you able to believe and receive right now that you are expecting a miracle and blessing overflow from God? How many of you also believing and receiving right now that your healing is on the way? Declare and decree this over your life right now that you will make because God is fighting for you and He will deliver you.

Chapter 10

Overcoming a Battle or Addiction

Isaiah 10:27; Psalms 120:1-2; Isaiah 54:17; Psalm 121:1-2; Philippians 4:19

I want to encourage you that you can overcome any battle or addiction you are going through right now. No matter what the devil and the doubters say about you, you will overcome this addiction. Your road to recovery might be tough but everything is going to be alright. God has you in the palm of His hands.

Don't focus on the negative comments and words that are headed in your direction; instead,, encourage yourself and speak over yourself that you will overcome, will recover, and be delivered from your battle with addiction.

I mentioned earlier in the book that a journey to recovery is not going to be easy at first, but if you continue to pray and have faith, if you stay focused and keep moving forward, you become successful. God has a bright future for you. God has something special, amazing, wonderful, marvelous, and awesome for you. Get ready because something big and great is about to take place in your life. You are moving forward and you are headed towards the purpose, vision, and plan that God has for you. Encourage yourself and say to yourself that you won't let your battle with addiction get you down. Also, encourage yourself and say to yourself that you will overcome your battle with addiction because God is doing something great and special in your life. Say to yourself, *"I am getting ready for it."* Always know that God is doing great and amazing things in your life. Get ready because big things are going to happen because we serve a God

Who is able to create miracles and blessings. Always know that we serve a God that can make a way, heal us, provide for us and deliver us.

This is your time to shine. Say to yourself that you will refuse to be held back by this battle with addiction. There are going to be times when the devil and the discouragers are going to come and and whisper negative comments about you. They are going to try to put you down because of your battle with addiction. But I want to remind you that GOD SEES THE BEST IN YOU. I want you encourage yourself that you are BEAUTIFUL, STRONG, MORE THAN A CONQUEROR, VICTORIOUS, a WINNER, CHAMPION, OVERCOMER AND SURVIVOR. I also want you to encourage yourself that you are HEALED, DELIVERED, RESTORED from this battle with addiction.

In Isaiah 10:27, the prophet declared, *"It shall come to pass in that day, that his burden shall be taken away from your shoulder and his yoke from your neck, and the yoke shall be destroyed because of the anointing oil."* [NKJV] That means the anointing of the Lord will destroy every yoke, evil plan, and distraction the devil is trying to attach to you. The anointing will destroy every negative comment and word that the doubters are saying about you.

Psalms 120:1-2 reads, *"In my distress I cried unto the Lord, and he heard me. Deliver my soul, O Lord, from lying lips, and from a deceitful tongue"*, and Isaiah 54:17 declares, *"No weapon formed against you shall prosper, and every tongue which rises against you in judgment You shall condemn"*.

Do not allow negative comments and words that negative people say to or about you stop you from reaching your destiny and goals. Be who God says you are. Always encourage yourself every day and keep declaring positive words over yourself. Always know that you are the child of the Most High God. Always know that you are beautiful, talented, a winner, a champion, and that you are healed, restored and delivered. Just keep staying in the faith and praying because God is going to work it out for you.

Psalms 121:1-2 reads, "*I lift up my eyes to the mountains where does my help come from? My help comes from the Lord, the Maker of heaven and earth*" (NIV) and Philippians 4:19 declares, "*And my God will meet all your needs according to the riches of his glory in Christ Jesus*" (NIV). These scriptures remind us that whatever we need, we can depend on God to provide. If you need a miracle, blessing, financial blessing and more, God got you. If you need to be restored, healed and delivered, trust in the Lord and keep praying because your harvest, your miracle, and your blessing is COMING!